DIABET

AND

KIDNEY DIET

2021

Eat healthy and prevent kidney failure: quick and delicious low-sodium and low-potassium recipes

LAURA FAYLER

Table of content

Lunch

LUNCH

Hearty Barley Risotto

Preparation time: 15 minutes

Cooking time: 60 minutes

Servings: 4-6

Ingredients:

- 1 carrot, peeled and chopped fine
- 1 cup dry white wine
- 1 onion, chopped fine
- 1 teaspoon minced fresh thyme or ¼ teaspoon dried
- 1½ cups pearl barley
- 2 ounces parmesan cheese, grated (1 cup)
- 2 tablespoons extra-virgin olive oil
- 4 cups chicken or vegetable broth

- 4 cups water
- Salt and pepper

Directions:

1. Bring broth and water to simmer in moderate-sized saucepan. Decrease heat to low and cover to keep warm.
2. Heat 1 tablespoon oil in a dutch oven on moderate heat until it starts to shimmer. Put in onion and carrot and cook till they become tender, 5 to 7 minutes.
3. Put in barley and cook, stirring frequently, until lightly toasted and aromatic, about 4 minutes. Put in wine and cook, stirring often, until fully absorbed, approximately two minutes.
4. Mix in 3 cups warm broth and thyme, bring to simmer, and cook, stirring intermittently, until liquid is absorbed and bottom of pot is dry, 22 to 25 minutes.
5. Mix in 2 cups warm broth, bring to simmer, and cook, stirring intermittently, until liquid is absorbed and bottom of pot is dry, fifteen to twenty minutes.
6. Carry on cooking risotto, stirring frequently and adding warm broth as required to stop pot bottom from becoming dry, until barley is cooked through, 15 to 20 minutes.
7. Remove from the heat, adjust consistency with remaining warm broth as required. Mix in parmesan and residual 1 tablespoon oil and sprinkle with salt and pepper to taste. Serve.

Nutrition: calories: 222 carbs: 33g fat: 5g protein: 6g

Hearty Freekeh Pilaf

Preparation time: 15 minutes

Cooking time: 60 minutes

Servings: 4-6

Ingredients:

- ¼ cup chopped fresh mint
- ¼ cup extra-virgin olive oil, plus extra for serving
- ¼ cup shelled pistachios, toasted and coarsely chopped
- ¼ teaspoon ground coriander
- ¼ teaspoon ground cumin
- 1 head cauliflower (2 pounds), cored and cut into ½-inch florets
- 1 shallot, minced
- 1½ cups whole freekeh
- 1½ tablespoons lemon juice
- 1½ teaspoons grated fresh ginger
- 3 ounces pitted dates, chopped (½ cup)
- Salt and pepper

Directions:

1. Bring 4 quarts water to boil in a dutch oven. Put in freekeh and 1 tablespoon salt, return to boil, and cook until grains are tender, 30 to 45 minutes. Drain freekeh, return to now-empty pot, and cover to keep warm.

2. Heat 2 tablespoons oil in 12-inch non-stick frying pan on moderate to high heat until it starts to shimmer.
3. Put in cauliflower, ½ teaspoon salt, and ¼ teaspoon pepper, cover, and cook until florets are softened and start to brown, approximately five minutes.
4. Remove lid and continue to cook, stirring intermittently, until florets turn spotty brown, about 10 minutes.
5. Put in remaining 2 tablespoons oil, dates, shallot, ginger, coriander, and cumin and cook, stirring often, until dates and shallot are softened and aromatic, approximately 3 minutes.
6. Decrease heat to low, put in freekeh, and cook, stirring often, until heated through, about 1 minute. Remove from the heat, mix in pistachios, mint, and lemon juice.
7. Sprinkle with salt and pepper to taste and drizzle with extra oil. Serve.

Nutrition: calories: 520 carbs: 54g fat: 14g Protein: 36g

Herby-Lemony Farro

Preparation time: 15 minutes

Cooking time: 40 minutes

Servings: 4-6

Ingredients:

- ¼ cup chopped fresh mint
- ¼ cup chopped fresh parsley
- 1 garlic clove, minced
- 1 onion, chopped fine
- 1 tablespoon lemon juice
- 1½ cups whole farro
- 3 tablespoons extra-virgin olive oil
- Salt and pepper

Directions:

1. Bring 4 quarts water to boil in a Dutch oven. Put in farro and 1 tablespoon salt, return to boil, and cook until grains are soft with slight chew, 15 to 30 minutes. Drain farro, return to now-empty pot, and cover to keep warm.
2. Heat 2 tablespoons oil in 12-inch frying pan on moderate heat until it starts to shimmer. Put in onion and ¼ teaspoon salt and cook till they become tender, approximately five minutes.

3. Mix in garlic and cook until aromatic, approximately half a minute. Put in residual 1 tablespoon oil and farro and cook, stirring often, until heated through, approximately two minutes.
4. Remove from the heat, mix in parsley, mint, and lemon juice. Sprinkle with salt and pepper to taste. Serve.

Nutrition: Calories: 243 Carbs: 22g Fat: 14g Protein: 10g

Dinner

DINNER

Simple Pork Stir Fry

Preparation time: 10 minutes

Cooking time: 15 minutes

Servings: 4

Ingredients:

- 4 ounces bacon, chopped
- 4 ounces snow peas
- 2 tablespoons butter
- 1-pound pork loin, cut into thin strips
- 2 cups mushrooms, sliced
- ¾ cup white wine
- ½ cup yellow onion, chopped
- 3 tablespoons sour cream

- Salt and white pepper to taste

Directions:

1. Put snow peas in a saucepan, add water to cover, add a pinch of salt, bring to a boil over medium heat, cook until they are soft, drain and leave aside.
2. Heat a pan over medium high heat, add bacon, cook for a few minutes, drain grease, transfer to a bowl and leave aside.
3. Heat a pan with 1 tablespoon butter over medium heat, add pork strips, salt and pepper to taste, brown for a few minutes and transfer to a plate as well.
4. Return pan to medium heat, add remaining butter and melt it. Add onions and mushrooms, stir and cook for 4 minutes.
5. Add wine, and simmer until it's reduced. Add cream, peas, pork, salt and pepper to taste, stir, heat up, divide between plates, top with bacon and serve.

Nutrition: calories 343 fat 31g carbs 21g protein 23g

Pork and Lentil Soup

Preparation time: 10 minutes, Time: 1 hour, Servings: 6

Ingredients:

- 1 small yellow onion, chopped
- 1 tablespoon olive oil
- 1 and ½ teaspoons basil, chopped
- 1 and ½ teaspoons ginger, grated
- 3 garlic cloves, chopped
- Salt and black pepper to taste
- ½ teaspoon cumin, ground
- 1 carrot, chopped
- 1-pound pork chops, bone-in 3 ounces brown lentils, rinsed
- 3 cups chicken stock
- 2 tablespoons tomato paste
- 2 tablespoons lime juice
- 1 teaspoon red chili flakes, crushed

Directions:

1. Heat a saucepan with the oil over medium heat, add garlic, onion, basil, ginger, salt, pepper and cumin, stir well and cook for 6 minutes.
2. Add carrots, stir and cook 5 more minutes. Add pork and brown for a few minutes. Add lentils, tomato paste and stock, stir, bring to a boil, cover pan and simmer for 50 minutes.

3. Transfer pork to a plate, discard bones, shred it and return to pan. Add chili flakes and lime juice, stir, ladle into bowls and serve.

Nutrition: calories 343 fat 31g carbs 21g protein 23g

Simple Braised Pork

Preparation time: 40 minutes

Cooking time: 1 hour

Servings: 4

Ingredients:

- 2 pounds pork loin roast, boneless and cubed
- 5 tablespoons butter
- Salt and black pepper to taste
- 2 cups chicken stock
- ½ cup dry white wine
- 2 garlic cloves, minced
- 1 teaspoon thyme, chopped
- 1 thyme spring
- 1 bay leaf
- ½ yellow onion, chopped
- 2 tablespoons white flour
- ¾ pound pearl onions
- ½ pound red grapes

Directions:

1. Heat a pan with 2 tablespoons butter over high heat, add pork loin, some salt and pepper, stir, brown for 10 minutes and transfer to a plate.

2. Add wine to the pan, bring to a boil over high heat and cook for 3 minutes.
3. Add stock, garlic, thyme spring, bay leaf, yellow onion and return meat to the pan, bring to a boil, cover, reduce heat to low, cook for 1 hour, strain liquid into another saucepan and transfer pork to a plate.
4. Put pearl onions in a small saucepan, add water to cover, bring to a boil over medium high heat, boil them for 5 minutes, drain, peel them and leave aside for now.
5. In a bowl, mix 2 tablespoons butter with flour and stir well. Add ½ cup of strained cooking liquid and whisk well.
6. Pour this into cooking liquid, bring to a simmer over medium heat and cook for 5 minutes. Add salt and pepper, chopped thyme, pork and pearl onions, cover and simmer for a few minutes.
7. Meanwhile, heat a pan with 1 tablespoon butter, add grapes, stir and cook them for 1-2 minutes. Divide pork meat on plates, drizzle the sauce all over and serve with onions and grapes on the side.

Nutrition: calories 320 fat 31g carbs 21g protein 23g

Fish Recipes

FISH & SEAFOOD

Dill Chutney Salmon

Preparation Time: 5 minutes

Cooking Time: 3 minutes

Serving: 2

Ingredients:

- Chutney:
- ¼ cup fresh dill
- ¼ cup extra virgin olive oil
- Juice from ½ lemon
- Sea salt, to taste
- Fish:
- 2 cups water
- 2 salmon fillets
- Juice from ½ lemon
- ¼ teaspoon paprika
- Salt and freshly ground pepper to taste

Direction:

1. Pulse all the chutney ingredients in a food processor until creamy. Set aside.

2. Add the water and steamer basket to the instant pot. Place salmon fillets, skin-side down, on the steamer basket. Drizzle the lemon juice over salmon and sprinkle with the paprika.
3. Secure the lid. Select the manual mode and set the cooking time for 3 minutes at high pressure.
4. Once cooking is complete, do a quick pressure release. Carefully open the lid.
5. Season the fillets with pepper and salt to taste. Serve topped with the dill chutney.

Nutrition: calories 636, 41g fat, 65g protein

Garlic-Butter Parmesan Salmon and Asparagus

Preparation Time: 10 minutes

Cooking Time: 15 minutes

Serving: 2

Ingredients:

- 2 (6-ounce / 170-g) salmon fillets, skin on and patted dry
- Pink himalayan salt
- Freshly ground black pepper, to taste
- 1 pound (454 g) fresh asparagus, ends snapped off
- 3 tablespoons almond butter
- 2 garlic cloves, minced
- ¼ cup grated parmesan cheese

Direction:

1. Prep oven to 400ºf (205ºc). Line a baking sheet with aluminum foil.
2. Season both sides of the salmon fillets.
3. Situate salmon in the middle of the baking sheet and arrange the asparagus around the salmon.
4. Heat the almond butter in a small saucepan over medium heat.

5. Cook minced garlic
6. Drizzle the garlic-butter sauce over the salmon and asparagus and scatter the parmesan cheese on top.
7. Bake in the preheated oven for about 12 minutes. You can switch the oven to broil at the end of cooking time for about 3 minutes to get a nice char on the asparagus.
8. Let cool for 5 minutes before serving.

Nutrition: calories 435, 26g fat, 42g protein

Lemon Rosemary Roasted Branzino

Preparation Time: 15 minutes

Cooking Time: 30 minutes

Serving: 2

Ingredients:

- 4 tablespoons extra-virgin olive oil, divided
- 2 (8-ounce) branzino fillets
- 1 garlic clove, minced
- 1 bunch scallions
- 10 to 12 small cherry tomatoes, halved
- 1 large carrot, cut into ¼-inch rounds
- ½ cup dry white wine
- 2 tablespoons paprika
- 2 teaspoons kosher salt
- ½ tablespoon ground chili pepper
- 2 rosemary sprigs or 1 tablespoon dried rosemary
- 1 small lemon, thinly sliced
- ½ cup sliced pitted kalamata olives

Direction:

1. Heat a large ovenproof skillet over high heat until hot, about 2 minutes. Add 1 tablespoon of olive oil and heat

2. Add the branzino fillets, skin-side up, and sear for 2 minutes. Flip the fillets and cook. Set aside.
3. Swirl 2 tablespoons of olive oil around the skillet to coat evenly.
4. Add the garlic, scallions, tomatoes, and carrot, and sauté for 5 minutes
5. Add the wine, stirring until all ingredients are well combined. Carefully place the fish over the sauce.
6. Preheat the oven to 450ºf (235ºc).
7. Brush the fillets with the remaining 1 tablespoon of olive oil and season with paprika, salt, and chili pepper. Top each fillet with a rosemary sprig and lemon slices. Scatter the olives over fish and around the skillet.
8. Roast for about 10 minutes until the lemon slices are browned. Serve hot.

Nutrition: calories 724, 43g fat, 57g protein

Grilled lemon pesto Salmon

Preparation Time: 5 minutes

Cooking Time: 10 minutes

Serving: 2

Ingredients:

- 10 ounces (283 g) salmon fillet
- 2 tablespoons prepared pesto sauce
- 1 large fresh lemon, sliced
- Cooking spray

Direction:

1. Preheat the grill to medium-high heat. Spray the grill grates with cooking spray.
2. Season the salmon well. Spread the pesto sauce on top.
3. Make a bed of fresh lemon slices about the same size as the salmon fillet on the hot grill, and place the salmon on top of the lemon slices. Put any additional lemon slices on top of the salmon.
4. Grill the salmon for 10 minutes.
5. Serve hot.

Nutrition: calories 316, 21g fat, 29g protein

Steamed Trout with Lemon Herb Crust

Preparation Time: 10 minutes

Cooking Time: 15 minutes

Serving: 2

Ingredients:

- 3 tablespoons olive oil
- 3 garlic cloves, chopped
- 2 tablespoons fresh lemon juice
- 1 tablespoon chopped fresh mint
- 1 tablespoon chopped fresh parsley
- ¼ teaspoon dried ground thyme
- 1 teaspoon sea salt
- 1 pound (454 g) fresh trout (2 pieces)
- 2 cups fish stock

Direction:

1. Blend olive oil, garlic, lemon juice, mint, parsley, thyme, and salt. Brush the marinade onto the fish.
2. Insert a trivet in the instant pot. Fill in the fish stock and place the fish on the trivet.
3. Secure the lid. Select the steam mode and set the cooking time for 15 minutes at high pressure.
4. Once cooking is complete, do a quick pressure release. Carefully open the lid. Serve warm.

Nutrition: calories 477, 30g fat, 52g protein

Roasted Trout Stuffed with Veggies

Preparation Time: 10 minutes, Time: 25 minutes Serving: 2

Ingredient:

- 2 (8-ounce) whole trout fillets
- 1 tablespoon extra-virgin olive oil
- ¼ teaspoon salt
- 1/8 teaspoon black pepper
- 1 small onion, thinly sliced
- ½ red bell pepper
- 1 poblano pepper
- 2 or 3 shiitake mushrooms, sliced
- 1 lemon, sliced

Direction:

1. Set oven to 425ºf (220ºc). Coat baking sheet with nonstick cooking spray.
2. Rub both trout fillets, inside and out, with the olive oil. Season with salt and pepper.
3. Mix together the onion, bell pepper, poblano pepper, and mushrooms in a large bowl. Stuff half of this mix into the cavity of each fillet. Top the mixture with 2 or 3 lemon slices inside each fillet.
4. Place the fish on the prepared baking sheet side by side. Roast in the preheated oven for 25 minutes
5. Pullout from the oven and serve on a plate.

Nutrition: calories 453, 22g fat, 49g protein

Lemony Trout with Caramelized Shallots

Preparation Time: 10 minutes

Cooking Time: 20 minutes

Serving: 2

Ingredients:

- Shallots:
- 1 teaspoon almond butter
- 2 shallots, thinly sliced
- Dash salt
- Trout:
- 1 tablespoon almond butter
- 2 (4-ounce / 113-g) trout fillets
- 3 tablespoons capers
- ¼ cup freshly squeezed lemon juice
- ¼ teaspoon salt
- Dash freshly ground black pepper
- 1 lemon, thinly sliced

Direction:

1. For shallots

2. Situate skillet over medium heat, cook the butter, shallots, and salt for 20 minutes, stirring every 5 minutes.
3. For trout
4. Meanwhile, in another large skillet over medium heat, heat 1 teaspoon of almond butter.
5. Add the trout fillets and cook each side for 3 minutes, or until flaky. Transfer to a plate and set aside.
6. In the skillet used for the trout, stir in the capers, lemon juice, salt, and pepper, then bring to a simmer. Whisk in the remaining 1 tablespoon of almond butter. Spoon the sauce over the fish.
7. Garnish the fish with the lemon slices and caramelized shallots before serving.

Nutrition: calories 344, 18g fat, 21g protein

Vegetables recipes

VEGETABLES

Egg White Frittata with Penne

Preparation time: 15 minutes

Cooking time: 30 minutes

Servings: 4 servings

Ingredients:

- Egg whites- 6
- Rice almond milk – ¼ cup
- Chopped fresh parsley – 1 tbsp.
- Chopped fresh thyme – 1 tsp
- Chopped fresh chives – 1 tsp
- Ground black pepper
- Olive oil – 2 tsp.
- Small sweet onion – ¼, chopped
- Minced garlic – 1 tsp
- Boiled and chopped red bell pepper – ½ cup
- Cooked penne – 2 cups

Directions:

1. Preheat the oven to 350f.
2. In a bowl, whisk together the egg whites, rice almond milk, parsley, thyme, chives, and pepper.

3. Heat the oil in a skillet.
4. Sauté the onion, garlic, red pepper for 4 minutes or until they are softened.
5. Add the cooked penne to the skillet.
6. Pour the egg mixture over the pasta and shake the pan to coat the pasta.
7. Leave the skillet on the heat for 1 minute to set the frittata's bottom and then transfer the skillet to the oven.
8. Bake the frittata for 25 minutes, or until it is set and golden brown.
9. Serve.

Nutrition: Calories: 170 kcal; Total Fat: 3 g; Saturated Fat: 0 g; Cholesterol: 0 mg; Sodium: 90 mg; Total Carbs: 25 g; Fiber: 0 g; Sugar: 0 g; Protein: 10 g

Spicy Corn and Rice Burritos

Preparation Time: 10 minutes

Cooking Time: 20 minutes

Servings: 4

Ingredients:

- 3 tablespoons of extra-virgin olive oil, divided
- 1 (10-ounce) package of frozen cooked rice
- 1½ cups of frozen yellow corn
- 1 tablespoon of chili powder
- 1 cup of shredded pepper jack cheese
- 4 large or 6 small corn tortillas

Directions:

1. Put the skillet in over medium heat and put 2 tablespoons of olive oil. Add the rice, corn, and chili powder and cook for 4 to 6 minutes, or until the ingredients are hot.
2. Transfer the ingredients from the pan into a medium bowl. Let cool for 15 minutes.
3. Stir the cheese into the rice mixture.
4. Heat the tortillas using the directions from the package to make them pliable. Fill the corn tortillas with the rice mixture, then roll them up.

5. At this point, you can serve them as is, or you can fry them first. Heat the remaining tablespoon of olive oil in a large skillet. Fry the burritos, seam-side down at first, turning once, until they are brown and crisp, about 4 to 6 minutes per side, then serve.

Nutrition: Calories: 386 Total fat: 21g Saturated fat: 7g Sodium: 510mg Phosphorus: 304mg Potassium: 282mg Carbohydrates: 41g Fiber: 4g Protein: 11g Sugar: 2g

Vegetable Confetti

Preparation Time: 25 minutes

Cooking Time: 15 minutes

Servings: 1

Ingredients:

- ½ red bell pepper
- ½ green pepper, boiled and chopped
- 4 scallions, thinly sliced
- ½ tsp. of ground cumin
- 3 tbsp. of vegetable oil
- 1 ½ tbsp. of white wine vinegar
- Black pepper to taste

Directions:

1. Join all fixings and blend well.
2. Chill in the fridge.
3. You can include a large portion of slashed jalapeno pepper for an increasingly fiery blend

Nutrition: Calories: 230 Fat: 25g Fiber: 3g Carbs: 24g Protein: 43g

Vegetable Green Curry

Preparation Time: 20 minutes Time: 20 minutes,Servings: 6

Ingredients:

- 2 tablespoons extra-virgin olive oil
- head broccoli, cut into florets
- 1 bunch asparagus, cut into 2-inch lengths
- tablespoons water
- tablespoons green curry paste
- 1 medium eggplant
- 1/8 teaspoon salt
- 1/8 teaspoon freshly ground black pepper
- 2/3 cup plain whole-almond milk yogurt

Directions:

1. Put olive oil in a large saucepan in a medium heat. Add the broccoli and stir-fry for 5 minutes. Add the asparagus and stir-fry for another 3 minutes.
2. Meanwhile, in a small bowl, combine the water with the green curry paste.
3. Add the eggplant, curry-water mixture, salt, and pepper. Stir-fry or until vegetables are all tender.
4. Add the yogurt. Heat through but avoid simmering. Serve.

Nutrition: Calories: 113 Total fat: 6g Saturated fat: 1g Sodium: 174mg Phosphorus: 117mg Potassium: 569mg Carbohydrates: 13g Fiber: 6g Protein: 5g Sugar: 7g

Rutabaga Latkes

Preparation Time: 15 minutes, Time: 7 minutes, Servings: 4

Ingredients:

- 1 teaspoon hemp seeds
- 1 teaspoon ground black pepper
- 7 oz. rutabaga, grated
- ½ teaspoon ground paprika
- 2 tablespoons coconut flour
- 1 egg, beaten
- 1 teaspoon olive oil

Directions:

1. Mix up together hemp seeds, ground black pepper, ground paprika, and coconut flour.
2. Then add grated rutabaga and beaten egg.
3. With the help of the fork combine together all the ingredients into the smooth mixture.
4. Preheat the skillet for 2-3 minutes over the high heat.
5. Then reduce the heat till medium and add olive oil.
6. With the help of the fork, place the small amount of rutabaga mixture in the skillet. Flatten it gently in the shape of latkes.
7. Cook the latkes for 3 minutes from each side.
8. After this, transfer them in the plate and repeat the same steps with remaining rutabaga mixture.

Nutrition: Calories 64, Fat 3.1, Fiber 3, Carbs 7.1, Protein 2.8

Glazed Snap Peas

Preparation Time: 10 minutes

Cooking Time: 5 minutes

Servings: 2

Ingredients:

- 1 cup snap peas
- 2 teaspoon Erythritol
- 1 teaspoon butter, melted
- ¾ teaspoon ground nutmeg
- ¼ teaspoon salt
- 1 cup water, for cooking

Directions:

1. Pour water in the pan. Add snap peas and bring them to boil.
2. Boil the snap peas for 5 minutes over the medium heat.
3. Then drain water and chill the snap peas.
4. Meanwhile, whisk together ground nutmeg, melted butter, salt, and Erythritol.
5. Preheat the mixture in the microwave oven for 5 seconds.
6. Pour the sweet butter liquid over the snap peas and shake them well.
7. The side dish should be served only warm.

Nutrition: Calories 80, Fat 2.5, Fiber 3.9, Carbs 10.9, Protein 4

Steamed Collard Greens

Preparation Time: 10 minutes

Cooking Time: 5 minutes

Servings: 2

Ingredients:

- 2 cups Collard Greens
- 1 tablespoon lime juice
- 1 teaspoon olive oil
- 1 teaspoon sesame seeds
- ½ teaspoon chili flakes
- 1 cup water, for the steamer

Directions:

1. Chop collard greens roughly.
2. Pour water in the steamer and insert rack.
3. Place the steamer bowl, add collard greens, and close the lid.
4. Steam the greens for 5 minutes.
5. After this, transfer the steamed collard greens in the salad bowl.
6. Sprinkle it with the lime juice, olive oil, sesame seeds, and chili flakes.
7. Mix up greens with the help of 2 forks and leave to rest for 10 minutes before serving.

Nutrition: Calories 43, Fat 3.4, Fiber 1.7, Carbs 3.4, Protein 1.3

VEGAN

Roasted Vegetable Mélange

Preparation time: 15 minutes

Cooking time: 25 minutes

Servings: 4

Ingredients:

- ½ cauliflower head, cut into small florets
- ½ broccoli head, cut into small florets
- 2 zucchinis, cut into ½-inch pieces
- 2 cups halved mushrooms
- 2 red, orange, or yellow bell peppers, cut into 1-inch pieces
- 1 sweet potato, cut into 1-inch pieces
- 1 red onion, cut into wedges
- 3 tablespoons olive oil
- 2 teaspoons minced garlic
- 1 teaspoon chopped fresh thyme
- Sea salt
- Freshly ground black pepper

Directions:

1. Preheat the oven to 400°f. Line a baking sheet with parchment paper and set aside.
2. In a large bowl, toss the cauliflower, broccoli, zucchini, mushrooms, bell peppers, sweet potato, onion, olive oil, garlic, and thyme until well mixed.
3. Spread the vegetables on the baking sheet and season lightly with salt and pepper. Roast until the vegetables are tender and lightly caramelized, stirring occasionally, 20 to 25 minutes. Serve.

Nutrition: calories: 183 fat: 11g carbohydrates: 20g protein: 5g

Couscous-Avocado Salad

Preparation time: 15 minutes

Cooking time: 10 minutes

Servings: 4

Ingredients:

- For the dressing:
- ¼ cup olive oil
- 2 tablespoons red wine vinegar
- 1 teaspoon minced garlic
- 1 teaspoon chopped fresh oregano
- Pinch red pepper flakes
- Sea salt
- Freshly ground black pepper
- For the salad:
- 1 cup couscous
- 2 cups halved cherry tomatoes
- ½ english cucumber, chopped
- 1 cup chopped marinated artichoke hearts
- 1 avocado, pitted, peeled, and chopped
- ½ cup crumbled feta cheese
- 2 tablespoons pine nuts

Directions:

1. To make the dressing:
2. In a small bowl, whisk together the olive oil, vinegar, garlic, oregano, and red pepper flakes. Season with salt and pepper and set aside.
3. To make the salad:
4. In a pot, bring 1½ cups of water to a boil. Stir the couscous into the boiling water and remove from the heat. Cover and let sit for 10 minutes. Fluff with a fork.
5. In a large bowl, toss together the couscous, cherry tomatoes, cucumber, artichoke hearts, avocado, feta cheese, and pine nuts. Add the dressing and toss to combine. Refrigerate for 1 hour and serve.

Nutrition: calories: 489 fat: 30g carbohydrates: 46g protein: 11g

Paprika Cauliflower Steaks with Walnut Sauce

Preparation time: 15 minutes

Cooking time: 30 minutes

Servings: 2

Ingredients:

- Walnut sauce:
- ½ cup raw walnut halves
- 2 tablespoons virgin olive oil, divided
- 1 clove garlic, chopped
- 1 small yellow onion, chopped
- ½ cup unsweetened almond milk
- 2 tablespoons fresh lemon juice
- Salt and pepper, to taste
- Paprika cauliflower:
- 1 medium head cauliflower
- 1 teaspoon sweet paprika
- 1 teaspoon minced fresh thyme leaves (about 2 sprigs)

Directions:

1. Preheat the oven to 350ºf (180ºc). Make the walnut sauce: toast the walnuts in a large, ovenproof skillet over medium heat until fragrant and slightly darkened, about 5 minutes. Transfer the walnuts to a blender.
2. Heat 1 tablespoon of olive oil in the skillet. Add the garlic and onion and sauté for about 2 minutes, or until slightly softened.
3. Transfer the garlic and onion into the blender, along with the almond milk, lemon juice, salt, and pepper. Blend the ingredients until smooth and creamy. Keep the sauce warm while you prepare the cauliflower.
4. Make the paprika cauliflower: cut two 1-inch-thick "steaks" from the center of the cauliflower. Lightly moisten the steaks with water and season both sides with paprika, thyme, salt, and pepper.
5. Heat the remaining 1 tablespoon of olive oil in the skillet over medium-high heat. Add the cauliflower steaks and sear for about 3 minutes until evenly browned. Flip the cauliflower steaks and transfer the skillet to the oven.
6. Roast in the preheated oven for about 20 minutes until crisp-tender. Serve the cauliflower steaks warm with the walnut sauce on the side.

Nutrition: calories: 367 fat: 27.9g protein: 7.0g carbs: 22.7g

Stir-Fried Eggplant

Preparation time: 15 minutes

Cooking time: 15 minutes

Servings: 2

Ingredients:

- 1 cup water, plus more as needed
- ½ cup chopped red onion
- 1 tablespoon finely chopped garlic
- 1 tablespoon dried italian herb seasoning
- 1 teaspoon ground cumin
- 1 small eggplant (about 8 ounces / 227 g), peeled and cut into ½-inch cubes
- 1 medium carrot, sliced
- 2 cups green beans, cut into 1-inch pieces
- 2 ribs celery, sliced
- 1 cup corn kernels
- 2 tablespoons almond butter
- 2 medium tomatoes, chopped

Directions:

1. Heat 1 tablespoon of water in a large soup pot over medium-high heat until it sputters. Cook the onion for 2 minutes, adding a little more water as needed.

2. Add the garlic, italian seasoning, cumin, and eggplant and stir-fry for 2 to 3 minutes, adding a little more water as needed.
3. Add the carrot, green beans, celery, corn kernels, and ½ cup of water and stir well. Reduce the heat to medium, cover, and cook for 8 to 10 minutes, stirring occasionally, or until the vegetables are tender. Meanwhile, in a bowl, stir together the almond butter and ½ cup of water.
4. Remove the vegetables from the heat and stir in the almond butter mixture and chopped tomatoes. Cool for a few minutes before serving.

Nutrition: calories: 176 fat: 5.5g protein: 5.8g carbs: 25.4g

Simple Honey-Glazed Baby Carrots

Preparation time: 15 minutes

Cooking time: 6 minutes

Servings: 2

Ingredients:

- 2/3 cup water
- 1½ pounds (680 g) baby carrots
- 4 tablespoons almond butter
- ½ cup honey
- 1 teaspoon dried thyme
- 1½ teaspoons dried dill
- Salt, to taste

Directions:

1. Pour the water into the instant pot and add a steamer basket. Place the baby carrots in the basket. Secure the lid. Select the manual mode and set the cooking time for 4 minutes at high pressure.
2. Once cooking is complete, do a quick pressure release. Carefully open the lid. Transfer the carrots to a plate and set aside. Pour the water out of the instant pot and dry it.
3. Press the sauté button on the instant pot and heat the almond butter. Stir in the honey, thyme, and dill.

4. Return the carrots to the instant pot and stir until well coated. Sauté for another 1 minute. Taste and season with salt as needed. Serve warm.

Nutrition: calories: 575 fat: 23.5g protein: 2.8g carbs: 90.6g

Quick Steamed Broccoli

Preparation time: 15 minutes

Cooking time: 0 minutes

Servings: 2

Ingredients:

- ¼ cup water
- 3 cups broccoli florets
- Salt and ground black pepper, to taste

Directions:

1. Pour the water into the instant pot and insert a steamer basket. Place the broccoli florets in the basket.
2. Secure the lid. Select the manual mode and set the cooking time for 0 minutes at high pressure. Once cooking is complete, do a quick pressure release. Carefully open the lid.
3. Transfer the broccoli florets to a bowl with cold water to keep bright green color. Season the broccoli with salt and pepper to taste, then serve.

Nutrition: calories: 16 fat: 0.2g protein: 1.9g carbs: 1.7g

Garlic-Butter Asparagus with Parmesan

Preparation time: 5 minutes

Cooking time: 8 minutes, Servings: 2

Ingredients:

- 1 cup water
- 1 pound (454 g) asparagus, trimmed
- 2 cloves garlic, chopped
- 3 tablespoons almond butter
- Salt and ground black pepper, to taste
- 3 tablespoons grated parmesan cheese

Directions:

1. Pour the water into the instant pot and insert a trivet. Put the asparagus on a tin foil add the butter and garlic. Season to taste with salt and pepper.
2. Fold over the foil and seal the asparagus inside so the foil doesn't come open. Arrange the asparagus on the trivet.
3. Secure the lid. Select the manual mode and set the cooking time for 8 minutes at high pressure. Once cooking is complete, do a quick pressure release. Carefully open the lid.
4. Unwrap the foil packet and serve sprinkled with the parmesan cheese.

Nutrition: calories: 243 fat: 15.7g protein: 12.3g carbs: 15.3g

Side dishes

SIDE DISHES

Lobster Tails with White Wine Sauce

Preparation Time:10 minutes

Cooking Time: 14 minutes

Serving: 4

Ingredients:

- `4 lobster tails, shell cut from the top
- `1/2 onion, quartered
- `1/2 cup butter
- `1/3 cup wine
- `1/4 cup honey
- `6 garlic cloves crushed
- `1 tablespoon lemon juice
- `1 teaspoon salt or to taste
- `Cracked pepper to taste
- `Lemon slices to serve
- `2 tablespoons fresh chopped parsley

Directions:

1. Place the lobster tails in the oven's baking tray.
2. Whisk rest of the Ingredients: in a bowl and pour over the lobster tails.
3. Press "power button" of air fry oven and turn the dial to select the "broil" mode.
4. Press the Time button and again turn the dial to set the cooking Time to 14 minutes.
5. Now push the temp button and rotate the dial to set the temperature at 350 degrees f.
6. Once preheated, place the lobster's baking tray in the oven and close its lid.
7. Serve warm.

Nutrition: Calories 340 Fat: 23.1g carbohydrate 20.4g protein 0.7g

Beet Salad with Parsley Dressing

Preparation Time 15 minutes

Cooking Time:15 minutes

Serving: 4

Ingredients:

- Black pepper and salt
- 1 clove of garlic
- 2 tbsp of balsamic vinegar
- 4 beets
- 2 tbsp of capers
- 1 bunch of chopped parsley
- 1 tbsp of olive oil

Directions:

1. Place bets on the Power XL Air Fryer Grill pan.
2. Set the Power XL Air Fryer Grill to air fry function.
3. Set Timer and temperature to 15 minutes and 3600F.
4. In another bowl, mix pepper, garlic, capers, salt, and olive oil. Mix well
5. Remove the beets from the Power XL Air Fryer Grill and place it on a flat surface.
6. Peel and put it in the salad bowl
7. Serve with vinegar.
8. Serving Suggestions: Dress with parsley mixture.
9. Directions: & Cooking Tips: rinse beets before cooking.

Nutrition: Calories: 185kcal, Fat: 16g, Carb: 11g, Proteins: 8g

Chicken Wings with Alfredo Sauce

Preparation Time:5 minutes

Cooking Time: 20 minutes

Servings: 4

Ingredients:

- 1 1/2 lb. chicken wings, pat-dried
- Salt to taste
- 1/2 cup Alfredo sauce

Directions:

1. Season the wings with salt. Arrange them in the greased air fryer basket, without touching and Air Fry for 12 minutes until no longer pink in the center. Work in batches if needed. Flip them, increase the heat to 390 F and cook for 5 more minutes. Plate the wings and drizzle with Alfredo sauce to serve.

Nutrition: Calories: 150 Carbs: 7 g Fat: 5 g Protein: 14 g

Zucchini Strips with Marinara Dip

Preparation Time:1 Hour and 10 Minutes

Cooking Time: 30 Minutes

Servings: 8

Ingredients:

- 2 zucchinis, sliced into strips
- Salt to taste
- 1 1/2 cups all-purpose flour
- 2 eggs, beaten
- 2 cups bread crumbs
- 2 teaspoons onion powder
- 1 tablespoon garlic powder
- 1/4 cup Parmesan cheese, grated
- 1/2 cup marinara sauce

Directions:

1. Season zucchini with salt.
2. Let sit for 15 minutes.
3. Pat dry with paper towels.
4. Add flour to a bowl.
5. Add eggs to another bowl.
6. Mix remaining Ingredients: except marinara sauce in a third bowl.
7. Dip zucchini strips in the first, second and third bowls.

8. Cover with foil and freeze for 45 minutes.

9. Add crisper plate to the air fryer basket inside the Power XL Grill.

10. Select air fry function.

11. Preheat to 360 degrees F for 3 minutes.

12. Add zucchini strips to the crisper plate.

13. Air fry for 20 minutes.

14. Flip and cook for another 10 minutes.

15. Serve with marinara dip.

Nutrition: Calories: 364 Fat: 35g Saturated Fat: 17g Trans Fat: 0g Carbohydrates: 8g Fiber: 1.5g Sodium: 291mg Protein: 8g

Roasted Garlic Dip

Preparation Time:10 minutes

Cooking Time: 20 minutes

Servings: 6

Ingredients:

- 1 head garlic
- ½ tablespoon olive oil

Directions:

1. Slice the top off the garlic.
2. Drizzle with the olive oil.
3. Add to the air fryer.
4. Set it to roast.
5. Cook at 390 degrees F for 20 minutes.
6. Peel the garlic.
7. Transfer to a food processor.
8. Pulse until smooth.

Nutrition: Calories: 207cal, Carbs: 17g, Protein: 9g, Fat: 12g.

Kohlrabi Chips

Preparation Time:10 minutes

Cooking Time: 20 minutes

Servings:10

Ingredients:

- 1lb kohlrabi, peel and slice thinly
- 1tsp paprika
- 1tbsp olive oil
- 1tsp salt

Directions:

1. Preheat the air fryer to 320 F.
2. Add all Ingredients: into the bowl and toss to coat.
3. Transfer kohlrabi into the air fryer basket and cook for 20 minutes. Toss halfway through.
4. Serve and enjoy.

Nutrition: Calories 108 Fat 1.4 g Carbohydrates 17.4 g Sugar 2.4 g Protein 7.3 g Cholesterol 0 mg

Daikon Chips

Preparation Time:10 minutes

Cooking Time: 16 minutes

Servings:6

Ingredients:

- 15 oz Daikon, slice into chips
- 1tbsp olive oil
- 1tsp chili powder
- 1/2 tsp pepper
- 1tsp salt

Directions:

1. Preheat the air fryer to 375 F.
2. Add all Ingredients: into the bowl and toss to coat.
3. Transfer sliced the daikon into the air fryer basket and cook for 16 minutes. Toss halfway through.
4. Serve and enjoy.

Nutrition: Calories: 207cal, Carbs: 17g, Protein: 9g, Fat: 12g.

SALAD

SALAD

Chicken Vegetable Salad

Preparation Time: 10 minutes

Cooking Time: 10 minutes

Servings: 4

Ingredients:

- 1 1/2 lbs. cooked chicken, cubed
- 1 cup cherry Red bell peppers, halved
- 4 small zucchinis, trimmed and sliced
- 8 oz. green beans, trimmed
- 1 tbsp. olive oil
- 1/2 small onion, sliced
- 2 tbsp. pesto
- Pepper
- Salt

Directions:

1. Add green beans into the boiling water and cook for 2 minutes. Drain well and transfer in large bowl.
2. Add remaining ingredients to the bowl and toss well.
3. Serve and enjoy.

Nutrition: Calories 369 Fat 12.3 g Carbohydrates 11.1 g Sugar 4.9 g Protein 53 g Cholesterol 133 mg Phosphorus: 110mg Potassium: 117mg Sodium: 75mg

Protein Packed Shrimp Salad

Preparation Time: 10 minutes

Cooking Time: 10 minutes

Servings: 4

Ingredients:

- 1 lb. shrimp, peeled and deveined
- 1 1/2 tbsp. fresh dill, chopped
- 1 tsp Dijon mustard
- 2 tsp fresh lemon juice
- 2 tbsp. onion, minced
- 1/2 cup celery, diced
- 1/2 cup mayonnaise
- Pepper
- Salt

Directions:

1. Add shrimp in boiling water and cook for 2 minutes. Drain well and transfer in large bowl.
2. Add remaining ingredients into the bowl and mix well.
3. Serve and enjoy.

Nutrition: Calories 258 Fat 11.9 g Carbohydrates 10.4 g Sugar 2.3 g Protein 26.5 g Cholesterol 246 mg Phosphorus: 135mg Potassium: 154mg Sodium: 75mg

Flavorful Pesto Chicken Salad

Preparation Time: 10 minutes

Cooking Time: 5 minutes

Servings: 4

Ingredients:

- 2 chicken breasts, cooked and shredded
- 1/2 cup parmesan cheese, shredded
- 1/4 cup mayonnaise
- 1/2 cup basil pesto
- 2 celery stalks, chopped
- Pepper
- Salt

Directions:

1. Add all ingredients into the mixing bowl and mix until well combined.
2. Serve and enjoy.

Nutrition: Calories 234 Fat 12.8 g Carbohydrates 4.3 g Sugar 1.1 g Protein 25 g Cholesterol 77 mg Phosphorus: 210mg Potassium: 107mg Sodium: 75mg

Bean and Pepper Soup with Coriander

Preparation time: 30mins

Cooking time: 20mins

Servings: 4

Ingredients:

- 1 onion
- 2 garlic cloves
- 2 tbsp. olive oil
- 2 red peppers
- 800 ml vegetable broth
- salt
- cayenne pepper
- Tabasco
- curry powder
- 2 cans kidney beans á 240 g
- 200 ml whipped cream at least 30% fat content
- 1 coriander

Directions:

1. Peel the onion and garlic, diced finely, and sauté in a saucepan with hot oil until translucent. Wash the bell peppers, cut in half, core, dice, and add. Sweat briefly and deglaze with the broth. Season with salt, cayenne pepper, curry, and Tabasco and simmer over medium heat for 10 minutes.
2. Pour the beans over a sieve, rinse with cold water and drain well.
3. Stir the cream with the beans into the soup and simmer for another 4 minutes.
4. Wash the coriander, shake dry, pluck the leaves off, and roughly chop.
5. Season the soup to taste, season again if necessary, pour into preheated bowls, and serve sprinkled with the coriander. Serve with a fresh baguette if you like.

Nutrition: Calories 357 kcal Protein 14 g Fat 22 g Carbohydrates 26 g

Hearty Vegetable Soup with Bacon

Preparation time: 12h

Cooking Time: 1 h 15 min

Servings: 4

Ingredients:

- 250 g dried kidney beans
- 150 g smoked bacon
- 1 large onion
- 2 garlic cloves
- 3 Red bell peppers
- 1 small savoy cabbage
- 4 carrots
- 2 tbsp. olive oil
- 1 ½ l meat soup
- salt
- pepper from the mill

Directions:

1. Soak the beans with cold water and leave overnight.
2. Drain the beans and cook them halfway through in fresh cold water for about 30–40 minutes.

3. In the meantime, dice the bacon. Peel onion and garlic and chop finely. Scald the Red bell peppers with boiling water for a few seconds, rinse, peel, quarter, core, and chop.
4. Clean and wash the cabbage, quarter lengthways, cut off the stalk, and cut the quarters crosswise into strips. Peel the carrots and cut into bite-sized pieces.
5. A sauce pan heats the olive oil and briefly brown the onions, garlic cloves, and bacon. Pour the meat stock. Add Red bell peppers, savoy cabbage strips, and carrots. Drain the beans and stir into the stock under the vegetables. Salt and pepper and let simmer on low heat for about 30 minutes.

Nutrition: Calories 567 kcal Protein 17 g Fat 40 g Carbohydrates 36 g

Mexican-Style Chicken and Vegetable Soup

Preparation time: 40 min,

Cooking Time: 2 h 10 min,

Servings: 4

Ingredients:

- 1 soup chicken
- 3 onions
- 2 carrots
- 150 g celery root
- 1 bay leaf
- 2 cloves
- 1 tsp peppercorns
- 1 tbsp. rapeseed oil
- 2 green peppers
- 1 red chili pepper
- 6 Red bell peppers
- 1 can of kidney beans
- 1 can corn
- salt
- pepper

Directions:

1. Wash the chicken soup and cover it with cold water in a saucepan that is large enough. Simmer. Boil.

Meanwhile, peel 2 onions, carrots, and celery, and roughly dice them.

2. Add the bay leaves, cloves, and peppercorns to the chicken and cook for about 2 hours, over medium heat. If necessary, skim off the foam occasionally and add water.

3. Take the chicken out of the soup. Strain the stock and measure 1 liter (otherwise use the remainder). Peel the chicken and the skin is removed. Have the meat cut into strips?

4. Peel the remaining onion and dice it. In a saucepan, sweat in hot oil until it is translucent. Pour the stock into it and bring it to a boil. In the meantime, wash, cut in half, clean and dice the peppers and chili. Scald the hot-water Red bell peppers, rinse, peel, quarter, core, and dice. Drain the beans and maize and add bell pepper, chili, Red bell peppers, and chicken to the soup.

5. For about 15 minutes, let everything simmer together. Season with pepper and salt and serve.

Nutrition: Calories/Energy: 69 Kcal, Protein: 5.13 g, Carbs: 7.87 g, Lipids: 2.01 g, Sodium: 347 mg, Calcium: 11 mg, Potassium: 153 mg, Phosphorous: 44 mg

Pesto Cucumber Tomato Salad

Preparation Time: 10 minutes

Cooking Time: 5 minutes

Servings: 6

Ingredients:

- 1 lb. cherry Red bell peppers, halved
- 1 tbsp. fresh lemon juice
- 1/4 cup pesto
- 1/3 cup onion, diced
- 1 cucumber, sliced
- Pepper
- Salt

Directions:

1. Add all ingredients into the large bowl and mix everything well.
2. Serve and enjoy.

Nutrition: Calories 206 Fat 17.6 g Carbohydrates 11.9 g Sugar 4.2 g Protein 3.4 g Cholesterol 3 mg Phosphorus: 110mg Potassium: 137mg Sodium: 85mg

ADDITIONAL RECIPES

ADDITIONAL RECIPES

Caprese Omelet

Servings: 1

Preparationtime:5minutes
Cooking Time:5 minutes;

Ingredients:

- 1/3 cup cherry tomatoes, halved
- 6 basil leaves, chopped
- 1/2 teaspoon sea salt
- 1/4 teaspoon cracked black pepper
- 1 tablespoon basil pesto, fresh
- 1 tablespoon olive oil and more for drizzling
- 3 eggs, pasture-raised
- 2 slices of fresh mozzarella cheese, full-fat
- 1 tablespoon grated parmesan cheese, full-fat

Directions:

1. Crack the eggs in a bowl and whisk until blended.
2. Place a small skillet pan over low heat, add oil and when hot, pour in eggs and bring the egg mixture to the center from pan from the sides with a spatula.

3. Then top one half of egg with half of the tomatoes, basil leaves, and cheeses and fold the other half of Caprese to cover this topping.
4. Cook omelet for 1 minute or until Caprese is set and then slide onto serving plate.
5. Drizzle Caprese with basil pesto and olive oil, top with remaining tomatoes and serve straightaway.

Nutrition: Calories: 533 cal, carbs: 4.9 g, fat: 43.2 g, protein: 30.8 g, fiber: 1.1 g.

Olive & Herb Focaccia

Servings: 4

Preparationtime:10minutes
Cooking Time:15 minutes;

Nutrition: Calories: 144 cal, carbs: 4.8 g, fat: 10.9 g, protein: 6.6 g, fiber: 3 g.

Ingredients:

- 1/4 cup sliced kalamata olives, fresh
- 1/3 cup and 1 tablespoon coconut flour
- 2 1/2 tablespoons psyllium husks
- 1 teaspoon baking powder
- 1/2 teaspoon salt
- 1 tablespoon minced fresh rosemary
- 1 tablespoon minced fresh sage
- 2 tablespoons olive oil
- 4 eggs, pasture-raised
- 2 tablespoons greek yogurt

Directions:

1. Set oven to 375 degrees F and let preheat.
2. In the meantime, crack eggs in a bowl, add yogurt and whisk until combined.

3. Place flour in another bowl, add psyllium husks, baking powder, and salt and stir until just mixed.
4. Add egg mixture and stir well until soft dough comes together.
5. Take a baking sheet, line with parchment paper, place dough on it and shape into a ½-inch thick rectangle.
6. Place a small saucepan over low heat, add salt, minced rosemary, and sage, 1 tablespoon olive oil and cook for 1 to 2 minutes or until fragrant.
7. Spoon this mixture over dough, then scatter with olive and drizzle with remaining oil and place baking tray into the heated oven.
8. Bake Focaccia for 15 minutes or until top is nicely golden brown and cooked through.
9. When done, slice to serve.

Savory Pancake

Servings: 1

Preparationtime:5minutesCooking Time:10 minutes;

Nutrition: Calories: 294 cal, carbs: 3.8 g, fat: 21.7 g, protein: 19 g, fiber: 1.5 g.

Ingredients:

- 2 tablespoons coconut flour
- 2 tablespoons chopped chives
- ½ teaspoon salt
- ¼ teaspoon cracked black pepper
- 1/4 teaspoon apple cider vinegar
- 1 tablespoon olive oil
- 3 eggs, pasture-raised
- 1/2 cup grated parmesan cheese, full-fat

Directions:

Separate egg yolks and egg whites in two bowls. Into egg whites, add vinegar and beat using a stand mixer until stiff peaks forms. Then fold in egg yolks, cheese, flour, chives, salt and black pepper with a whisker. Place a small skillet pan over medium heat, add oil and when hot, pour in pancake mixture. Cook for 3 minutes or until bottom sets and bubbles appear on top. Turn on broiler, place pan containing pancake into the broiler and cook for 3 to 5 minutes or until top is nicely golden brown. When done, slide pancake to a serving plate and serve.

Mushroom Risotto

Servings: 2

Preparationtime:20minutes
Cooking Time:20 minutes;

Nutrition: Calories: 287 cal, carbs: 11.3 g, fat: 24.4 g, protein: 8 g, fiber: 3.4 g.

Ingredients:

- 6 cups riced cauliflower, fresh
- ½ cup dried porcini mushrooms, organic
- 4 cups fresh wild mushrooms, chopped
- ¼ cup chopped fresh parsley
- 1 small white onion, peeled and sliced
- 1 teaspoon minced garlic
- 1 tablespoon lemon juice
- ¼ cup and 2 tablespoons olive oil
- ½ cup heavy whipping cream, full-fat
- ⅔ cup grated parmesan cheese, full-fat
- ¾ cup chicken broth, pasture-raised

Directions:

1. Pour chicken broth in a bowl, add porcini mushrooms and let soak for 15 minutes.

2. Then place a large skillet pan over medium-high heat, add ½ cup oil and when hot, add onion and garlic.

3. Cook for 5 to 8 minutes or until nicely golden brown, then wild mushrooms and cauliflower rice and stir well.

4. Add soaked porcini mushrooms along with their liquid, season with salt, stir in cream and cook risotto for 8 to 10 minutes or until cauliflower is tender.

5. Remove pan from heat, drizzle remaining olive oil and lemon juice over risotto, sprinkle with cheese and stir until combined.

6. Serve straightaway.

Pesto Pull-Apart Bread

Servings: 12

Preparationtime:10minutes

Cooking Time:60 minutes;

Nutrition: Calories: 236 cal, carbs: 10.4 g, fat: 19 g, protein: 10 g, fiber: 6.7 g.

Ingredients:

- 1/2 cup pecans
- 1 bunch fresh basil
- 2 cups arugula
- 2 teaspoons minced garlic
- ½ teaspoon sea salt
- ½ teaspoon ground black pepper
- 2 teaspoons lemon zest
- 1/4 cup olive oil
- 1 tbsp lemon juice
- 1/2 cup grated parmesan cheese, full-fat
- 12 sourdough baguettes dough, low-carb

Directions:

1. Set oven to 325 degrees f and let preheat.
2. In the meantime, prepare pesto and for this, place pecans, basil, arugula, garlic, salt, black pepper, lemon zest, and lemon juice.
3. Pulse for smooth, then gradually blend in olive oil until combined and tip pesto into a bowl.
4. Place dough onto a clean working space, shape into 12 portions, then place 1 tablespoon prepared pesto into the center of each dough and roll into balls.
5. Take a large skillet pan, grease with olive oil and arrange the prepare dough balls in the bottom of the pan in a circular pattern.
6. Top with parmesan cheese until all dough balls are covered and then place pan into the heated oven.
7. Bake for 50 to 60 minutes or until dough balls are cook through and the top is golden brown.
8. When done, remove the pan from oven and let rest for 5 minutes.
9. Serve straightaway.

DESSERT RECIPES

DESSERTS

Mint Banana Chocolate Sorbet

Preparation time: 4 hours & 5 minutes

Cooking time: 0 minutes

Servings: 1

Ingredients:

- 1 frozen banana
- 1 tablespoon almond butter
- 2 tablespoons minced fresh mint
- 2 to 3 tablespoons dark chocolate chips (60% cocoa or higher)
- 2 to 3 tablespoons goji (optional)

Directions:

1. Put the banana, butter, and mint in a food processor. Pulse to purée until creamy and smooth. Add the chocolate and goji, then pulse for several more times to combine well.
2. Pour the mixture in a bowl or a ramekin, then freeze for at least 4 hours before serving chilled.

Nutrition: calories: 213 fat: 9.8g Protein: 3.1g Carbs: 2.9g

Pecan and Carrot Cake

Preparation time: 15 minutes

Cooking time: 45 minutes

Servings: 12

Ingredients:

- ½ cup coconut oil, at room temperature, plus more for greasing the baking dish
- 2 teaspoons pure vanilla extract
- ¼ cup pure maple syrup
- 6 eggs
- ½ cup coconut flour
- 1 teaspoon baking powder
- 1 teaspoon baking soda
- ½ teaspoon ground nutmeg
- 1 teaspoon ground cinnamon
- 1/8 teaspoon sea salt
- ½ cup chopped pecans
- 3 cups finely grated carrots

Directions:

1. Preheat the oven to 350ºf (180ºc). Grease a 13-by-9-inch baking dish with coconut oil. Combine the vanilla extract, maple syrup, and ½ cup of coconut oil in a large bowl. Stir to mix well.

2. Break the eggs in the bowl and whisk to combine well. Set aside. Combine the coconut flour, baking powder, baking soda, nutmeg, cinnamon, and salt in a separate bowl. Stir to mix well.

3. Make a well in the center of the flour mixture, then pour the egg mixture into the well. Stir to combine well.

4. Add the pecans and carrots to the bowl and toss to mix well. Pour the mixture in the single layer on the baking dish.

5. Bake in the preheated oven for 45 minutes or until puffed and the cake spring back when lightly press with your fingers.

6. Remove the cake from the oven. Allow to cool for at least 15 minutes, then serve.

Nutrition: calories: 255 fat: 21.2g protein: 5.1g carbs: 12.8g

Raspberry Yogurt Basted Cantaloupe

Preparation time: 15 minutes

Cooking time: 0 minutes

Servings: 6

Ingredients:

- 2 cups fresh raspberries, mashed
- 1 cup plain coconut yogurt
- ½ teaspoon vanilla extract
- 1 cantaloupe, peeled and sliced
- ½ cup toasted coconut flakes

Directions:

1. Combine the mashed raspberries with yogurt and vanilla extract in a small bowl. Stir to mix well.
2. Place the cantaloupe slices on a platter, then top with raspberry mixture and spread with toasted coconut. Serve immediately.

Nutrition: calories: 75 fat: 4.1g protein: 1.2g Carbs: 10.9g